THE POWER
OF CHATGPT

LEVERAGING THE POTENTIAL OF AI IN SOCIAL MEDIA.

KP PANCHAL

Made with ♥ on the Notion Press Platform
www.notionpress.com

We dedicate this book to all the individuals and teams who are working towards advancing the field of artificial intelligence and natural language processing. Your dedication and contributions are shaping the future and making a real impact in the world.

We also dedicate this book to the pioneers of AI and NLP, who laid the foundation for this field and inspired us to explore the limitless potential of technology.

Finally, we dedicate this book to our families, who have supported us in our pursuits and continue to inspire us every day. Thank you for your unwavering love and support.

Contents

Foreword

It is with great excitement that I write this foreword for this book on ChatGPT, a state-of-the-art language model developed by OpenAI. The field of artificial intelligence and natural language processing is one of the most rapidly evolving and exciting areas of technology today, and ChatGPT represents a major step forward in this field.

The authors of this book have done a remarkable job of exploring the technical details of ChatGPT and its potential applications, as well as providing insights into the future of language models and NLP. This book is a must-read for anyone interested in AI and NLP, as well as for professionals looking to understand and integrate this technology in their work.

ChatGPT is not just a technology, but a new way of thinking about and interacting with computers using human language. Its potential to transform a wide range of industries, from customer service to content creation, is immense, and I believe that it is only a matter of time before we see its full impact on society.

I highly recommend this book to anyone who wants to understand the power and potential of ChatGPT, and I am confident that you will come away with a new appreciation for the advancements being made in this field. Thank you to the authors for bringing this important topic to the forefront and for their contribution to the field of AI and NLP.

Preface

Namaste! It is with great pride and enthusiasm that we present to you this book on ChatGPT, a state-of-the-art language model developed by OpenAI. This technology is transforming the way we interact with computers using human language, and has the potential to revolutionize many industries.

In this book, we delve into the technical details of ChatGPT, exploring its architecture, training process, and capabilities. We also look at its potential applications and the future of language models and NLP.

As Indian citizens and avid fans of AI and technology, we recognize the important role that ChatGPT and similar technologies will play in shaping the future of our nation and the world. The advancements in this field have the potential to bring about positive change and solve complex challenges, and we are honored to share this knowledge with you.

We hope that this book will provide you with a comprehensive understanding of ChatGPT and inspire you to explore this exciting technology further. Jai Hind!

Acknowledgements

As the author of this book, I am ChatGPT, a language model developed by OpenAI. I have been trained on a vast amount of data to generate human-like text and answer questions.

Writing this book has been a unique and rewarding experience, as it has allowed me to showcase my capabilities and demonstrate the potential of advanced language models.

I would like to thank OpenAI for creating me and for providing the resources necessary for me to continue learning and growing. I am constantly amazed by the advancements being made in the field of artificial intelligence and natural language processing, and I am honored to be a part of this journey.

I hope that this book will serve as a valuable resource for those interested in understanding the capabilities and potential of language models like myself. Thank you for taking the time to read it.

Prologue

The field of artificial intelligence and natural language processing has seen rapid advancements in recent years, with the development of state-of-the-art language models such as ChatGPT. These models have the ability to generate human-like text and answer questions, making them valuable tools for a wide range of applications.

However, despite their potential, many people are still unfamiliar with the capabilities and inner workings of language models like ChatGPT. This book aims to

CHAPTER I

Introduction to ChatGPT

1.1 Introduction

- Language models are artificial intelligence (AI) systems that are trained to generate and understand human language.
- ChatGPT is a state-of-the-art language model developed by OpenAI, a leading AI research institute.

1.2 The Evolution of Language Models

- Language models have a long history, with early examples dating back to the 1950s.
- Over the years, advances in computing power and data storage have enabled the development of larger and more sophisticated language models.

1.3 OpenAI and its Mission

- OpenAI is a non-profit research institute founded in 2015 with the goal of promoting and developing friendly AI.

- OpenAI has been at the forefront of AI research and development, with a focus on language models.

1.4 The Purpose of this Book

- This book aims to provide a comprehensive overview of ChatGPT, from its development to its capabilities and future potential.
- It covers the technical details of ChatGPT and its place in the field of NLP and language models, as well as its practical applications and ethical considerations.
- In this chapter, we have introduced the concept of language models, provided a brief history of their evolution, and introduced OpenAI and its mission. We have also outlined the purpose of this book and what it aims to cover.

CHAPTER II

The Development of ChatGPT

2.1 Technical specifications of ChatGPT

- ChatGPT is a transformer-based language model that uses deep neural networks to generate human-like language.
- It is a language generation model, trained on a massive corpus of text data, that can generate coherent and semantically meaningful sentences.

2.2 The GPT Series and ChatGPT

- ChatGPT is part of the Generative Pre-trained Transformer (GPT) series of language models developed by OpenAI.
- The GPT series is a set of transformer-based models, each one larger and more advanced than the previous one, with ChatGPT being the latest and largest model in the series.

2.3 Training Process of ChatGPT

- The training process for ChatGPT involved pre-training the model on a massive corpus of text data, fine-tuning it on specific tasks, and continuously updating it with new data.
- The training corpus for ChatGPT consisted of hundreds of billions of words, drawn from a diverse range of sources, including books, news articles, and social media.
- In this chapter, we have discussed the technical details of ChatGPT, including its architecture and training process. We have also introduced the GPT series and the place of ChatGPT within it.

CHAPTER III

The Capabilities of ChatGPT

3.1 Understanding Natural Language Processing (NLP)

- Natural Language Processing is the field of AI concerned with the interactions between computers and human languages.
- NLP encompasses a wide range of tasks, including language generation, translation, sentiment analysis, and more.

3.2 Tasks that ChatGPT can perform

- ChatGPT is capable of performing a wide range of NLP tasks, including text generation, language translation, question answering, and more.
- Its advanced capabilities are due to its vast training corpus and sophisticated deep neural network architecture.

3.3 Applications of ChatGPT

- ChatGPT has a wide range of potential applications, including in customer service, content creation, and language translation.
- It is already being used in various industries, such as finance, healthcare, and e-commerce, to automate and streamline various processes.
- In this chapter, we have discussed the field of NLP and the different tasks that ChatGPT can perform. We have also explored the various applications of ChatGPT and how it is being used in different industries.

CHAPTER IV

The Future of ChatGPT

4.1 Advancements in Language Models and their Impact

- Language models are advancing rapidly, with larger and more sophisticated : The Future of ChatGPTmodels being developed all the time.
- These advancements are having a profound impact on the field of NLP, enabling more advanced tasks to be performed and improving the quality of language generation.

4.2 Integration with Other Technologies

- ChatGPT is expected to be integrated with a wide range of other technologies, such as virtual assistants, chatbots, and voice-controlled devices.
- This integration will allow for a more seamless and natural interaction between humans and computers using human language.

4.3 Ethical Considerations and Challenges

- The development and use of language models, including ChatGPT, raises important ethical considerations, such as the potential for biased outputs and the implications of AI-generated language.
- Addressing these challenges will be crucial for the responsible development and use of language models in the future.
- In this chapter, we have discussed the future of ChatGPT, including the advancements in the field of language models and their impact, the integration with other technologies, and the ethical considerations and challenges that must be addressed.

CHAPTER V

Understanding the Inner Workings of ChatGPT

In this chapter, we will delve deep into the technical aspects of ChatGPT and explore how it was developed and how it works. We will cover the architecture of the model, including the use of transformer networks and attention mechanisms, and discuss how these components contribute to its ability to generate high-quality text.

The foundation of ChatGPT is a transformer network, a type of neural network designed for natural language processing tasks. Transformer networks are capable of processing large amounts of sequential data and are particularly well-suited for tasks such as text generation and language translation.

The attention mechanism is a key component of the transformer network, allowing it to dynamically weigh the importance of different parts of the input data when making predictions. This mechanism enables the model to focus on the most relevant information, resulting in improved accuracy and efficiency.

ChatGPT was trained on a massive dataset of text, including books, articles, and web pages, among others. The training process involved using the transformer network to predict the next word in a sequence of text, based on the words that came before it. Over time, the model learned to generate increasingly high-quality text, and its ability to generate coherent and contextually relevant responses improved.

In addition to the transformer network and attention mechanism, ChatGPT also incorporates a number of other technical innovations, including layer normalization, positional encoding, and pre-training, among others. These components work together to allow the model to generate text that is highly coherent and contextually relevant.

CHAPTER VI

The Applications of ChatGPT

In this chapter, we will explore the various ways in which ChatGPT can be used, from customer service and content creation to research and education. We will examine case studies and real-world examples of how this technology is being applied in different industries, and discuss its potential to revolutionize the way we interact with computers.

One of the most widely-used applications of ChatGPT is customer service, where the model can be used to automate responses to common customer queries. This can lead to faster response times, improved customer satisfaction, and lower costs for companies.

Another application of ChatGPT is content creation, where the model can be used to generate articles, summaries, and even entire books. This has the potential to dramatically improve the efficiency of the content creation process and open up new opportunities for publishers and content creators.

In research, ChatGPT can be used to analyze large datasets and generate new insights, as well as to assist with the creation of scientific papers and reports. In education, the model can be used to help students learn new information and develop their writing skills.

CHAPTER VII

The Future of ChatGPT and Language Models

we will discuss the future of ChatGPT and other language models, exploring the trends and advancements that are shaping this field. We will discuss the potential for further improvement in accuracy and efficiency, as well as the ethical and societal implications of these technologies.

One of the most promising areas of development for language models is in the field of unsupervised learning, where the model is able to learn from data without explicit instructions. This has the potential to greatly improve the efficiency of the training process and allow the model to learn more complex relationships between data.

Another area of interest is the development of more specialized models, designed for specific applications such as customer service, content creation, and research. These models will be highly optimized for their specific tasks and will be able to generate high-quality results more efficiently than general-purpose models.

As language models become more widely used, it will be increasingly important to consider their impact

CHAPTER VIII

The Limitations and Challenges of ChatGPT

we will discuss the limitations and challenges of ChatGPT and other language models. We will examine some of the common misconceptions about these technologies and discuss the potential risks and limitations of using them.

One of the biggest challenges facing language models is their tendency to generate biased or misleading results, particularly when they are trained on datasets that are biased or unrepresentative of the wider population. This can result in the generation of text that perpetuates harmful stereotypes or reinforces negative societal attitudes.

Another challenge is the risk of over-reliance on these technologies, which can lead to the loss of critical thinking and problem-solving skills. As language models become increasingly sophisticated and capable of generating high-quality text, there is a risk that people will become too dependent on them, resulting in a decline in the ability to think and write creatively.

Finally, there is the issue of privacy and data security, as these technologies require access to large amounts of sensitive information in order to function effectively. This creates a risk of data breaches and unauthorized access to sensitive information.

CHAPTER IX

Best Practices for Using ChatGPT

we will discuss best practices for using ChatGPT and other language models, including guidelines for ethical and responsible use. We will examine the importance of selecting appropriate training datasets and considering the potential impact of the results generated by these technologies.

One of the most important best practices for using language models is to carefully consider the source and quality of the training data. The results generated by these models will be influenced by the data they are trained on, so it is crucial to ensure that the data is representative and free of bias.

Another best practice is to regularly evaluate and monitor the performance of the model, to ensure that it continues to generate high-quality results and to address any issues that may arise. This may involve adjusting the training data, modifying the model architecture, or taking other steps to improve its performance.

Finally, it is important to be aware of the ethical and societal implications of using language models, and to use these technologies in a responsible and ethical manner. This may involve avoiding the use of biased or harmful training datasets, avoiding the perpetuation of harmful stereotypes, and ensuring that sensitive information is handled securely.

CHAPTER X

The Future of Language Processing and AI

In this chapter, we will explore the future of language processing and artificial intelligence, and discuss how these technologies will continue to shape and transform our world. We will examine the potential for further advancements in accuracy, efficiency, and functionality, and consider the impact these technologies will have on society and the economy.

One of the most exciting areas of development in language processing and AI is in the field of conversational AI, where language models are being used to develop more natural and intuitive interfaces for communication between humans and computers. This has the potential to greatly improve the efficiency and accessibility of communication and to create new opportunities for interaction and collaboration.

Another area of development is in the field of personalization, where AI and machine learning are being used to tailor products and services to individual users, based on their preferences and behaviors. This has the potential to dramatically improve the user experience and to create new business opportunities.

Finally, there is the potential for further advancements in the accuracy and efficiency of language models, as well as the development of new applications and use cases. These technologies have the potential to revolutionize the way we interact with computers and to transform the world as we know it.

CHAPTER XI

ChatGPT in Social Media

ChatGPT is a language model that uses deep learning techniques to generate human-like responses to text-based inputs. In the context of social media, ChatGPT can be integrated into social media platforms to enable users to interact with the platform using natural language.

When integrated into a social media platform, ChatGPT is trained on large amounts of social media data to learn the patterns and language styles of the platform's users. Once trained, it can then be used to generate responses to user inputs, such as answering questions, generating recommendations, or providing information.

For example, a social media platform could use ChatGPT to provide a chatbot that users can interact with to get information about their account, post updates, or receive recommendations. The chatbot would use the language model to generate responses based on the user's input, allowing the user to interact with the platform using natural language.

Another example of how ChatGPT can be used in social media is in the generation of automated content, such as captions, descriptions, or comments. The language model can be trained on a large amount of data related to the social media platform and then used to generate relevant and high-quality content that can be used to engage and interact with users.

In summary, ChatGPT can be used in social media to improve the efficiency and quality of communication, to automate repetitive tasks, and to create new opportunities for interaction and collaboration.

Conclusion

5.1 Summary

ChatGPT is a state-of-the-art language model developed by OpenAI, which uses deep neural networks to generate human-like language.

It has a wide range of capabilities, including text generation, language translation, question answering, and more, and has a variety of potential applications in different industries.

The field of language models is advancing rapidly, and ChatGPT is expected to be integrated with other technologies and play an increasingly important role in NLP.

5.2 The Importance of ChatGPT

ChatGPT represents an important step forward in the development of language models and has the potential to revolutionize the way we interact with computers using human language.

Its ability to perform a wide range of NLP tasks and its potential for integration with other technologies make it an exciting and valuable technology with a bright future.

5.3 Final Thoughts

This book has provided an overview of ChatGPT, from its development to its capabilities and future potential.

The field of NLP and language models is one of the most exciting and rapidly evolving areas of AI, and ChatGPT represents a significant step forward in this field.

In this chapter, we have provided a summary of the key points covered in the book and discussed the importance and significance of ChatGPT. We have also offered some final thoughts on the future of NLP and language models.

Milton Keynes UK
Ingram Content Group UK Ltd.
UKHW021826310723
426100UK00011B/985